Copyright © 2018 by Runnell Townsend Jr
All rights reserved. This book or any portion thereof may not be reproduced or used in any manner whatsoever without the express written permission of the publisher except for the use of brief quotations in a book review.

Printed in the United States of America

First Printing, 2018

ISBN-13: 978-0692092248

13347 S. Mackinaw Ave
Chicago, IL 60633

Logo created by: Increase Branding and Design

www.MyLoveEmpowers.com

Letters for my Daughter

If ever my thoughts could warm your heart

Written by

Runnell Townsend Jr.

"I hope this book encourages fathers to foster better relationships with their kids and to infect the world with love, especially their daughters."

"Through life's experiences and lessons I've learned, these are few of the teachings I envision to be perpetuated in my daughter's life.

Runnell Townsend Jr.

Contents

1. What it Felt Like When You Were Born
2. Rock Bottom
3. Right Can Go Wrong
4. Loving One Another, Even When It Hurts
   a. Peace, Love, and Happiness
5. Know Your Worth
6. Love Isn't Materialistic
7. Your Love

As a student of life, I dedicate this book to the art of loving. Love is dynamic and conquers all. If left with unfilled capacity, love can purify the hearts of all those that allow it in.

I also dedicate this book to my parents, Runnell Townsend Sr. and Michelle Lori Townsend. These two have shown my siblings and I what stern and tender love for their kids looks like. Though none of us are the same, the beauty in how they loved each of us differently according to who we are, was beautiful in its own art.

Last but not least, I dedicate this book to my pretty, beautiful, and gorgeous daughter, Mia. She is the epitome of love. Her love is tenacious, resilient and infectious. Because of her, I now know the true depths of love.

Chapter 1: What it Felt Like When You Were Born

Of all the things in life that I've faced head on, to this date, fatherhood is what consumes my mind. I was scared, I was nervous, and I had no clue how to feel. Was I going to be a great father? A great husband? A great example of what to look for in a man? What lessons would I teach as the provider and the primary male figure in your life? How soft or how hard do I need to be on a little girl?

All I knew was tough love growing up with four boys and one girl, a military father, and a mother that had to be a soldier while pop was at war. Despite how detail-oriented I usually am and how thoroughly I plan everything out when it comes to my life's goals, for once, I was lost with no answers.

My plan of action was to always be present, follow your mother's lead, and step in when I needed to. I had no clue! What it felt like when you were born is that I now have two girls to look out for in my life; two girls that will forever depend on Daddy; two girls to live for; two girls that Daddy couldn't fail or let down. Oh, how the pressure built up by the months, the weeks, the days, the hours, the minutes. All the way until Mommy began pushing around 11:30 AM and the doctor determined that we needed to conduct a C-section around 4:30 PM after nonstop pushing. My heart dropped, and I had an empty feeling of helplessness. There was nothing I could physically do to help Mommy, yet all that time, I wished I could take her pain while she delivered you. It was impossible.

I sat next to Mommy in the surgery room while she lay awake, her stomach with an incision for your exit. She laid there cold and shivering. I sat there without site beneath her chest, due to a curtain blocking us. As helpless as I felt, I asked for warm blankets to keep her warm while we held hands. She looked into my eyes with worry and anxiety, ready to meet you... our daughter. I gazed back with confirmation that everything would be OK. Then, they pulled you from her tummy and we heard a subtle cry. There you were - a purple baby. The doctor then took you to a separate table and cut your umbilical cord. They immediately brought you back to Daddy to hold while they put Mommy back together.

    In that moment, I wasn't overjoyed. Although I was happy, I couldn't help but feel saddened that your mother was unable to be the first to hold you due to the circumstances. I felt helpless. I never spoke about how terrible I felt even though I had no choice in that. The only option I had was to lean you over so that she could see you before being put back together. She smiled, but was still worried… all she wanted was you. I don't even think she cared that her tummy was still open. So, quickly after our acquaintance, we sat in a room by ourselves for a while until Mommy came in. I made a few promises to you that I'll share with you one day. At 6:03 PM on 2/10/2014, my life changed, and I became a new man - a better man, a selfless man, a proud man, a humbled man. Still, as prideful and as armored as I was, admittedly, I felt helpless, when you were born. For this reason, I dedicate my life to giving you most things you want and everything you need in life.

Before you were born, I made a promise to you, to the world. I didn't break my promise because I did my best. I loved as hard as I could even though I still raise you in a home separate than that of your mother's. God willing, he intended a lifestyle for the three of us that we didn't envision. However, I'm still grateful for a daughter with a full and loving heart. Your Mommy and I were so hurt that our love for one another faded so we loved you as hard as we could so that you didn't have to feel the pain we felt. The product of that love resulted in a beautiful little girl that saw no wrong or evil in any person that you encountered. At the age of three, you speak love - an innocent love that I personally envied. Witnessing your love encouraged me to love how you love. You taught me to love unconditionally and without judgement. I'm thankful for the blessing you've bestowed upon me at such a young age.

My promise to you:

Dear Mia Amor Townsend,

You're only 5 ½ months still inside your Mommy's tummy, but I'm writing this letter to you to make a promise to you in front of the world. I promise to love you with all my heart and to treat your mother how I would want your future husband to treat you. I will show you how a man is supposed to treat a woman by example of how I treat Mommy. I promise to take you on dates and open your doors so that your angelic hands won't have to endure any abuse that a man's should. I promise to tell you every day that I love you and to hold you tight until I give another young man my blessing to take your hand in marriage. I promise to let Mommy show you how to be a wonderful woman as she herself is, for I can only show you how to be loved and what kind of man to look for. I promise not to be so strict that you become secretive and drift away; I will give you space and let you grow up accordingly. I promise to love you the best way I know how, and most importantly, I will be the best man I can be for you and Mommy for as long as God allows me to lead the way. I can't wait to see and hold you Angel Baby!

Love, Daddy

It's ironic that in a moment of complete, blissful happiness, I wrote that small letter to you as a covenant to the world to hold me accountable as a father. I didn't realize that a few years later, I'd be writing a book to you with a few other letters to express my love for you after such a life impacting experience your mother and I chose to go through.

Call Me Baby...

There's no better feeling than the love from your seed

That unconditional love that even a man unwarrantedly needs

Mia... no, call me baby!

A hug from her father, a kiss from his lips

A fatherless little girl? She'll never miss

Dad... no, call me Daddy!

If ever a man were to feel unwanted, there's always that one little girl

that he knows, no matter what, he'll be her world

Mia... no, call me baby!

It is Daddy's job to always speak in love. What else would she

know when she goes to seek her hub?

Dad… no, call me Daddy!

Mia's my little girl and she'll always be my baby

Dad I am, but I prefer to be called Daddy.

There was a time in your life that inspired me to write this poem. If I ever called you by your first name, you took offense because you were so used to me calling you "baby." So, being the smart little girl that you are, to pay me back, you'd call me "dad," and as you could imagine, I took offense as well. When I would call you "Mia," you'd firmly tell me "No! Call me baby." It was cute and hilarious. When you'd call me "dad," I'd tell you, "No, call me Daddy."

A few months later, you and I were having a conversation through Facetime. You were talking to your mother, having a side conversation and apparently, something smelled bad. I recall asking you, "Who are you talking to?" You responded, "Daddy pooped." I knew that you were blaming whatever smell you and your mother encountered on me, but I intentionally acted like you said, "Daddy Pooh." I got excited and said, "Aw that's my new nickname?" With you seeing my excitement, you went with it because you didn't want to disappoint me. Eventually, our pet names changed to Baby Pooh" and "Daddy Pooh."

You changed my life, you saved my life, and now, I dedicate my life to you. I promise not only to be the best father I can, but to be the best man I know how to be by learning to be the best co-parent I can, and leaving a legacy on this earth so that even when I'm gone, you'll have a financial legacy that you can pass along to your kids, and your kids' kids, and their kids' kids. This legacy began to manifest the day you were born.

Chapter 2: Rock Bottom

Often, we as humans have visions and goals for our lives that we intend to happen just as we imagined. Naturally, it never happens the way we intend so we must be prepared for the unforeseen circumstances and obstacles that come our way. You need to be prepared to roll with the punches, endure the storms, and ride the waves. If you remain tenacious and diligent with whatever you aspire to do in life, you'll always conquer. Take those unplanned occurrences and build character, shape yourself into a better person, and a better woman.

The best thing that can happen to a man is heartbreak and hitting rock bottom. One happening, or both happening simultaneously will define and chisel the character of him tremendously. This state of discomfort creates dialogue between you and you. For me, I experienced rock bottom just before your birth. It was the hardest time of my life as the provider, the protector, and the man in your life. I decided to interrupt my studies in my Doctoral program for a job opportunity that was promised to me in the Chicagoland area. I couldn't pass it up. Love motivated me. Love made me leap and bound on faith.

As I took this leap of faith and started a new life with your Mommy, it came to my attention that grant funds were no longer being approved for the upcoming fiscal year for that company. With a newly acquired apartment in a new area, a new fiancé, a new baby on the way, and a Master's with an incomplete Doctoral degree... I was jobless. It would have been easy to have gone back to my program two hours away, teaching at the University for income... but Mommy would have gone through her pregnancy without me. Perseverance was of the utmost importance and needed to be put into practice during this time. I struggled to look for a job in the summer months. I took out countless loans and maxed out all my credit cards so that that Mommy and I didn't have to burn through the money that she was able to set aside. We had plans to use those funds for a home to raise you in. It was my vision, my dream for my family: my wife and my unborn daughter.

There were hard decisions that needed to be made. Mommy worked tirelessly during her entire pregnancy with you and I admired and respected her for that. We didn't see eye-to-eye on quite a few decisions, but it was all for the betterment of our family, I assure you.

After almost eleven months in Chicago, Daddy landed a job in the transportation industry working four days on and three days off from 4 AM to 4 PM. Daddy also worked the night shift because you were only two months old at the time. It was tough for Mommy and Daddy. We pressed through and bought our first home in July, a month after officially getting married. We were planning our actual wedding ceremony for the following year. Eventually, I lost my job because I struggled with arriving on time at 4 AM those days and it caught up to me. However, blessings come in disguise and a month later, I found a job in my field! All the hardships took a toll on Mommy and Daddy, however. We didn't communicate well nor did we see eye-to-eye, but we tried our best to make things work. Eventually, after hitting rock bottom financially along with the hardships in our marriage, everything led to a mutual heartbreak that neither of us could no longer endure. February of that next year, it was time to part ways which meant raising you in two homes. We couldn't agree on what that looked like or how that would impact taking care of you financially or parenting-wise. We spent over a year and a half in the court system trying to figure out parenting time. After all that time, we still didn't have it figured out, but all I knew was that I needed you.

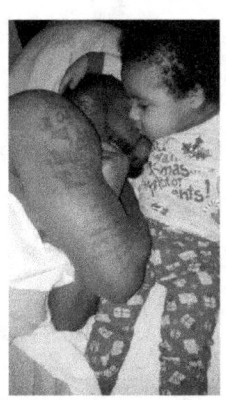

I need you...

I need you because I'm lost
I need you to be found
I need you to keep sound
I need you...
Because when I'm with you,
I'm level headed and my feet are planted on the ground.
I need you like you need me
It isn't an obsession, it's a reciprocated love that no words can describe.
I need you because when I'm without you, my rhythmic calibrations are off and I need you so they can vibe
You complete me,
You give me life, and something to live for.
You are my reason, you are my "why."
No matter my trials, no matter my discomfort,
I need you to keep me going
Keep me going when I'm out of air and without gas
I need you when I'm going through it because you remind me that it won't last
There's always light in the darkness and
I bled for you, I cried for you… I would have died for

you

*And now that I'm out,
I thank you because you being my "why" was all I needed from you.*

I learned a lot about love during this time. I learned a lot about myself and the Universe. Leave everything negative behind. The same energy you put into dying needs to be reciprocated and put into energy to live. I discovered my purpose through pain and channeled my energy so that I wasn't defeated mentally, spiritually, and physically. When you do it from the heart, it'll become infectious. Whatever you put your mind to, spread your love across the world. Let love deflect hate, invite peace, and deter anger. Do it from your heart and all will be well. Your heart is pure and abundant. I promise it will always be enough.

Love Betrayal...

How love betrayed me? Love is honest, love is clear, love is true, love is kind, and most of all, love is blind. We choose to love and we choose to fall. Our choice in the Who is most important of them all; how we love them is as important as the who. Even then, it's a choice. But, that all depends on our perception of love.

Is love one term with one definitive description? What does it mean to the person loving and to the person receiving? Is it adequate? Does it fill your voids? Does it fill your heart with joy?

There is no specific definition, but we learn to love how people need to be loved. It's a language, learn it! Otherwise, there is a defect in the line of communication for love partners. Some messages will never get through to the other simply because it was never received - it was an undelivered message. This process of loving must be reciprocated equally. It's a choice. Invest your heart into another's so that the expense, or loss, creates an equilibrium in both hearts. In essence, this means nothing was ever lost nor gained. Rather, it was an experience of growth for people with equally invested loves.

Love is the only true "why" that exists. No matter what we do in life, there's a reason behind it, some are more passionate than others, but overall, we do things because we'd love to see the result we are looking for. Hence, it's the true why. We never live for ourselves. We wake up by the grace of God and we push though for God, but also subconsciously for someone we love here on this earth. It is the only true why that exists. It's not perceived - it is purposeful, it is obvious, it is warranted, it is conscience, and it is selfless. Love is everything we are not.

All the while, I never wanted to stop dreaming of love. I call my dream, the "miscarried dream."

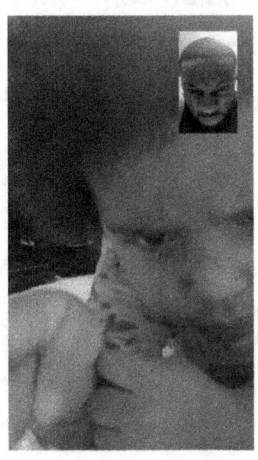

Miscarried Dream...

Often, we have these infatuated dreams based on the outer shell of what we view: "I want a life like that, a car like that, a house like that, hair like that, a body like that, skin like that, money like that, a man like that, a woman like that, etc.," but in reality, we don't have a clue of what's inside that shell. Do we really want something we know nothing about? Dr. King had a dream, and I believe it was heaven sent that I had a dream as well which I pursued with everything in me. Over the years, it took some time for me to realize that Dr. King's dream was his to live for. My dream was false and misleading, so I thought. Dr. King knew he envisioned a specific outcome for America, and God gave him the will to carry on, helping it manifest. He did the same for mine. My dream didn't unfold how I planned it and I'm not sure that Dr. King's did either. But, it did for God. See, it wasn't on our time... it was on His time and although what we had in mind didn't work out how we dreamt, it worked out how God intended. Sacrifice, struggle, pain, and grit; Dr. King's legacy lives on and his name is forever remembered. Now, I'm not putting myself on his level, but my dream has a similar purpose. I chased it, and it was worth it. I *didn't know the magnitude of what my dream meant, but my blessing from that dream was you, my sweet baby girl. Now, God has set on my heart that with my love for you, I have to change the world. Two dreams, two men, just to be better, two different generations with a different purpose yet a part of the same team. All this time, I thought I had a miscarried dream.*

Make no mistake, baby girl. Yes, I had a dream and pursued it with every ounce of love within me, but the vision I had was with a different purpose than I imagined. Had my experience with your mother not happened, I wouldn't love how I love, I wouldn't be as driven as I have become, and most importantly, I wouldn't appreciate my moments with you as much as I do now.

Love is beautiful, but love can be painful. You will be betrayed by love. Your heart will be broken. It doesn't have to be with a romantic partner, but also by friends and family. It's a part of life and helps build character while teaching us important lessons of life. Learn the language of love. Become bilingual in its language so that you can speak to the world. Some of my biggest struggles were having conflict between my mind and my heart. Find a balance, pray to God and let him lead the way. Only life's experiences will teach you how to listen to one or the other. Most importantly, when your heart is broken, there's an art to waiting and allowing your wounds to heal. Know what that is for your sanity and the comfort of your soul.

Around your third birthday, I encountered a joke on social media that prompted parents to ask their kids a few questions. It went like this:

WITHOUT prompting, ask your child these questions and write EXACTLY what they say.

My interview with Mia (freshly 3 in February)

1. What is something I say a lot

Mia: "I love you."

2. What makes me happy?

Mia: "When I make you rings and necklaces."

3. What makes me sad?

Mia: "When I don't come to your house."

4. How tall am I?

Mia: "So big because you can even touch the sky."

5. How old am I?

Mia: (shrugs shoulders) "Maybe you're 06 (zero-six)."

6. What's my favorite thing to do?

Mia: "To pick up Kiki and Lili and go to McDonalds play place and to give me chocolate milk, and go to the gym."

7. What makes you proud of me?

Mia: "Because I'm your baby."

8. What is my favorite food?

Mia: "Chicken nuggets, and chorizo, and eggs."

9. *If I could go anywhere, where would I go?*
Mia: "Gym, outside to walk to the museum, and to the zoo."
10. *Do you think you could live without me?*
Mia: *(shakes her head no)* I'd rather go with Mommy and Daddy
11. *How do I annoy you?*
Mia: "When you squish me."
12. *What is my favorite TV show?*
Mia: "Chicago Fire."
13. *Who do I have a crush on?*
Mia: "Sofia and me."

What stood out to me the most from this exercise was that your personality is out of this world! I've noticed that you've been playing and tricking me to make me feel good by telling me what I want to hear. Under no circumstances are you sad when you "don't come to my house;" you're always happy with Mommy and Daddy, probably a bit happier with Mommy. I found it hilarious reading this a year later because you do similar things to ensure that Daddy feels secure as Daddy. I appreciate that type of love so much. When I asked you what I tell you the most, it made me realize that no matter what Mommy and I didn't get right, we've done a damn good job at teaching you how to love.

How to Love...

The question on how to love is what truly determines vacancy to our hearts.
How do you love?
How were you taught to love?
Were you given hugs and kisses?
If so, from whom?
Was it your father?
Your mother?
What did that look like for you?
How did it feel?
With every relationship, we have to learn how someone is loved.

We might not respond in the manner of which the other will receive.
Must I paint you a picture?
Do I need to sing you a song?
Do I need to crochet the world with my hands?
Must I do nothing but listen?
How am I to love you effectively, genuinely, and wholeheartedly so that the love I give you is abundant and fills every void or empty space you'll ever need?
Sometimes, my love won't be enough.
I'm OK with that because I know you have the direction and guidance to receive what you need appropriately.
I'll never be sorry for loving you.
I'll never feel that I neglected to love you enough.
I'll never wonder if my love was enough,
Because when my heart stops beating for you on this earth,
I know that you will know how I loved, and it was everything in me.
There was no infatuation with how I loved you.
If ever love emulated that of our flowing blood, then may you never be empty, and may my love live on forever within you.

Learn how you need to be loved, learn how you give love, but most importantly, be attentive to how others need and want to be loved. It will take you a long way in life because everyone loves differently. Respect that and understand that; don't allow a skewed perception because of your perspective. Be open to love and be open to different angles of life for yours isn't the only. Become one with the Universe.

Sync...

In sync with the Universe.
To be in sync with the Universe,
You receive what you give.
Love or hate is what you choose to live.
I'm in sync!
In sync with love and the life I've chosen.
I'm blessed with a life of love and a daughter that's golden.
In sync!
I'm in sync with the stars and the beauty of the Universe.
As I'm blessed, I'll bless thee, to never be deemed a curse.
The worst!
I'm in sync with the Universe.
My peace, my love, my happiness... I'll never let be taken.
Neither my Holy Spirit, my mentality, nor my heart will ever be forsaken.
I'm in sync with the Universe.
You are my priority,
You are my everything. Because of you,
I am everything!

Wear many hats, yet under each, let your heart remain. For every blessing that you receive, the pressure intensifies because neither are for you, but rather are intended for the world. You're nothing without God, but with Him, you are everything. With that perspective, the world will receive our love.

Chapter 3: Right can Go Wrong

Right can go wrong
When you're in it too long
When your love is so gone.
On and on,
Your love is so gone.
When you're doing it wrong,
You love too long, doing it right
But they are the wrong... one.
Even though right can go wrong
And with you loving the wrong... one
You'll figure out what's right
You become immune to the wrong that it feels so right, that
when right comes around, if feels so wrong.
But, deep down inside you know they are the wrong... one

So, you proceed in your journey because you must learn on your own and in due time, we always resort back to what we were shown.

I've learned that right can go wrong to only reveal what we've already known

And now, I'm blown.

My world upside down; my life, inside out.

What is this all about?

What am I to learn from this?

What am I to do?

For the first time in forever, I am lost

I admit.

They say, "let go and let God,"

I pray every day because my life feels robbed.

Maybe not robbed, maybe it has just begun.

Even when there's so much wrong, sometimes, we have to lead the way by showing what's right.

Baby Pooh, no matter how good we try to be in this world, sometimes our intentions aren't perceived how we intended them to be. Never judge someone based on their mistakes. Instead, uplift them and infect them with the love that Mommy and Daddy have instilled in you. Pay attention to the heart because not everything is as plain and clear as it may seem. Always stray clear from making conclusions based on the surface.

Just as an iceberg may seem minute and diminutive to the human eye, beneath the surface is a gigantic monument with so many different conditions and structures that contribute to its massive figure. When we meet a person, sometimes we make assumptions based on their outer appearance without knowing who they really are. If you see the tip of the iceberg as a handsome, successful man, be sure to undergo thorough research. Underneath that handsome man can be deceit, hate, false charm, evilness, selfishness, and many other bad qualities that may not compliment who you are. Be sure to detect qualities underneath that iceberg that show hard work, dedication, loyalty, failure, past rejections, sacrifices, persistence, discipline, and all the qualities that you envision to compliment your beautiful life from your life partner.

Mia, when Daddy refers to failure, and rejections, I personally believe that a man that has experienced these life experiences has built character. Knowing how a man has overcome trials and tribulations can define him as man and the kind of man he will grow into. When you see glamor on the surface, take your time to know how he got there. Do not judge him, but reflect on how he treats triumph and disaster.

If there are no perceived failures, how are we growing as an individual? What are we learning from? If we haven't been rejected, how then will we know how to push harder? How will we know how to re channel rejection and convert that feeling into fire to succeed with our goals? Any person that can't admit to failure simply hasn't learned a precious gift in life: humility.

Perception is more important than what may be seen as clarity or certainty. Some people in this world will experience pain and sit in it so long that they become consumed with victimization and pity. In contrast, other folks will take that pain and use it to push harder, to reach further, and to dig deeper so that they one day have a testimony that speaks to the world and inspires them to get through their pain. How will you perceive pain? Will you let is destruct you? Will you allow it to make you stronger? Allow pain to live in you - be vulnerable to the feeling, but don't let it sit too long. The human body is a mysterious creation by God and I'd hate to encourage you to soak in pain or to ignore it altogether. You need to have balance and allow your body to undergo the process it needs to in order for you to operate at your fullest potential.

A lot of the time, when right goes wrong, we experience this pain, allowing ourselves to sit and sulk too long. It is OK to feel the pain for a bit and endure the process you need to go through to not feel what you feel any longer. The key, however, is to recognize what put you in the state that you are in. Thus, you need to learn from it, grow from it, and grow out of it. You will become a better person after it.

Alignment Versus Parallel...

You'd think the two are quite similar when referencing definitions.
Again, refrain from looking at the surface of things.
Look deeper!
An adjustment to a line would define and alignment.
Confinement? No.
Having the same direction or course without converging defines parallel.
Right direction? Can't tell.
If you think about life and love, the two may seem to be aligned and parallel.
We often reference this as being on "the same page."
My life has oftentimes seemed on the "right path," but was never parallel.
Parallel to what? Parallel to who?
A car has wheels that are always parallel, but periodically, they need an alignment.
What does that do?
See, sometimes we can be on the right path and going in the direction we are intended for... however, because of our human nature and our ability to make mistakes, we unknowingly stray away.
It's never a bad thing to deter from your intended destination.
A lot of time, it's divine intervention that requires you to go

off the path so that you can experience life, test your learnings, chisel your character, and define who you are. Without labels, it's hard to establish a tea flavor until the bag is put in hot water, revealing its flavor. What flavor are you? You are sweet, you are authentic, and you are exceptional. There is no one like you on the market; in fact, you are not for sale. You are rare in form!

When you go astray and need your periodic alignment, seek God first, refuel your soul, rejoice with family, be still, and spend time with yourself.

Stay parallel to your vision and goals, but be wise to know that parallel isn't always straightforward. Sometimes we cruise in autopilot and forget the tune ups and alignments. There's a difference.

    A new beginning to my life. As Mommy and I decided to live separately, I had to start over without causing a drastic change in your lifestyle. Thank God for family during hard times. For a short period of your life (maybe less than a year), whenever you spent your time with Daddy, we stayed with family in Bolingbrook, Illinois. It was hard for me to support myself, pay court fees, and provide for you all at the same time. You call them Uncle Malt, and Titi Rose. This was, admittedly, one of the hardest times of my life as a man.

    I was no longer in my own home, I had to bring you to a foreign home an hour away to a bedroom that I was renting at Titi and Uncle's house, to provide a roof over our heads. Despite how thankful I was, I was still so embarrassed and humbled as a grown man. Daddy had a plan, I just wasn't sure how it was going to pan out. God had all the answers for me, though. For about seven months, this was our routine when we had Daddy/Daughter time.

During this time, I got closer to God. I was spending my Sundays at Church, my Wednesdays at Bible study, and my mornings and nights praying on my hands and knees. I felt that everything that was right was going wrong. I had hit rock bottom again... only this time, it was spiritually, or so I thought. Every time I went to church or Bible study, I found myself being touched by the word - so touched that I was uncontrollably emotional at every service. At the time, I was embarrassed. As a man, I was taught that showing emotions and letting tears flow like that is usually a sign of weakness. I don't agree with that, but the pride in me still makes me feel "less of a man" sometimes. I'm only being candid and transparent with you so that I can accurately express how I felt at the time. My heart was heavy.

I'll never forget a warm day in September of 2016 when I went to my home church of Salem Baptist Church (House of Hope). The Pastor's message during this Bible study spoke about life's trials and tribulations and how we seek Christ when we are going through bad times. But, when things are good, we often forget Him and fail to thank Him. He began to deeply express specific hardships we as humans go through and the message resonated so much to what I was going through, that I began to cry. I immediately tried to hide my tears, but as he spoke more, my tears became heavy like waterfalls. I couldn't control it - all I could think about was you, my life, my marriage, and how I was going to make it through.

The tears kept coming, so I held my head down to hide, but with my heart so heavy, it was obvious that I was emotional. I'll never forget that there was a woman next to me. She never said a word to me nor did she ever ask me what was wrong. This lady simply put her hand on my back, consoling me as I cried my tears. After about 5 minutes, she began to pray for me. She prayed for exactly what I needed, and I had never known this woman a day of my life. Did the tears stop? No, they actually came down heavier. She prayed, I prayed, we prayed together. Eventually, I got up and left because the tears wouldn't stop. For me, this was a sign.

God was letting me know how much I needed Him and how much He wanted me. My next few church services, I sat in the back, yet these emotions continued for the next couple of months until I surrendered to God. When you were with Daddy on my weekends, we would usually go to church if we were in town. At one specific service, the Word was speaking to me to join the church, and so I did. I walked up to the altar with you in my arms, my eyeballs sweating, and I surrendered to my gut, my holy spirit that had been speaking to me. From that point forward, I decided to never ignore my holy spirit again. I began to live more righteous and focus on my spiritual growth.

    As I focused on my spiritual growth and getting my life back together, God showed me that by being obedient and choosing to grow in Christ as a person, I could begin to receive the blessings He had been waiting to bless me with. In August of 2016, I was no longer in my home with you and Mommy, not by choice, but those were the circumstances. Six months later, God blessed me with a new house. Despite everything on this earth that I didn't and still don't know, all I knew is that you needed me, and I needed you. I dedicated my life to being there for you, even if it meant sacrificing where I wanted to truly live. I knew that with your mother and I not being together anymore, she'd want to stay in the Hegewisch neighborhood to raise you because her entire family is there on her side.

    God blessed me to be able to buy a new house on the other side of the neighborhood and being exactly 4 minutes and 33 seconds from you put peace in my heart. I knew that co-parenting would be easier... I also knew that when Mommy and I started new lives with new people that it would be complicated at first, but we would eventually grow into a loving and caring village that got along for you.

    Everything that God set on my heart to do, I did. I continue to pursue and listen to my holy spirit wholeheartedly. It has never steered me wrong, and as I began to establish my life and set a new foundation, I promised I wouldn't do it without God this time. With God's grace, family support, financial assistance from Nana and Poppa, and the moral support from friends and family, we got through it. All my years I had been praying for peace, love and happiness, I had finally gotten it. God has a funny way of giving us what we pray for.

    I want to share a sacred moment with you that brought tears to my eyes each time we experienced this. For the months that we lived in Bolingbrook, I wasn't in a situation to provide you with toys and other luxuries that you would normally have in the comfort of your own home. One of your favorite places to go was McDonalds Play place, so I took you there often to play with other kids and have a quick meal on my dinner days. In addition to that, Daddy wasn't able to provide toys, so you and I would go to Walmart and play with accessible toys in the toy section. You loved it, but I felt ashamed and it broke my heart. We switched Walmart's often so that the staff members didn't recognize us as we spent time in the toy isle a few days of the week.

    After dropping you off by your mother's, I'd cry on the way home because I felt ashamed in a way because I had to take you to Walmart to play with toys. Regardless of how I felt, I continued to take you because it made you happy when we did those kinds of things. During that time, I began to teach you something that I still hold dear to my heart and no person on this earth knew the meaning until now. When I say, "If we have each other..." you would respond with "We have everything we want." I needed to drill that inside of you because regardless of our circumstances and no matter what we go through in life, if we have each other, then we are complete. The toys don't matter and the material things that God blesses us with can easily be taken, but this bond, this love, can never be taken away. My love for you and yours for me can never be broken by any person, any judge, any law, any amount of money, or anything else on this Universe. No other person on the face of this earth will ever share the love you and I have with one another. I may have to share your heart in different ways, but there is and always will be a space in your heart that only I, your father, can fill.

Chapter 4: Loving One Another, Even When It Hurts (Peace, Love, and Happiness)

To let love live and to let love grow,
See, I have been to the land where love was rich and love was poor.
But see, that didn't deter me from thinking that love wasn't real no more.
Because if I thought love doesn't exist,
Then I'm out my wits,
Because my lord Jesus Christ invented it.
Love is God and God is love, so it's only right that as a man I persist,
To build a family like this.
The foundation of your home should be for love to consist.
Don't let hate coexist,
Let love circumvent
I speak from wisdom baby girl,

this love, mutual love, its heaven sent.
Recognize the gift.
It's about compromise - give, take, maneuver, shift.
When he falls and she falls, together you both lift.
Be her rock, be their rock, and when he's too busy being strong, know when to soften him up with a kiss.
Sometimes, the man must let his woman be the rock, switch.
Be strong enough to know when it's her turn to be the fist.
Be it as it may, you might just have to deliver her that angelic Kiss.
Be firm, be soft, be tender
When you both say, "I do," you both will surrender.
Not even realizing you both are winners.
Winners to love, winners to marriage, winners as one.
A journey to forevership as a unit has begun.
Always, always honor your covenant.
There will be struggles, there will be pain
But never forget the love in your veins.
Love isn't easy, I would never proclaim,
But it's a beautiful thing when love don't change.
Love each other when it hurts
That's the key to the game.

    I was to love your mother rich or poor, in sickness and in health, and I did. So, why didn't our marriage work? Simply put, I didn't love her how she needed to be loved and it wasn't reciprocated. This caused turmoil with our peace, our love, and our happiness. Though I recognized our marriage was off, I needed to find a solution. Coming from family that had trying, but withstanding marriages, I had a decent idea of how to make it work: we needed more time with one another alone, more church services, professional counseling, and more understanding of one another's upbringings. We needed to understand how we received loved, and how we gave it. I bought a few books I thought that we could read together. Ultimately, we had different ideas of what our family looked like.

    My entire life, I had a vision of a family and success, so much so that I was willing to make sacrifices along the way to achieve them. Oh, when I met your mother, my life changed. She was the most beautiful thing on the face of this earth, and I knew that I had to make her mine so, I did. Despite our differences in how we were raised and what our vision of what a healthy relationship looked like, all we knew was that we loved one another and we were inseparable. We overlooked major differences that later became detrimental to our relationship - we fought, we made up, and we fought more. Eventually, it became a norm for us. I prayed daily for peace, love, and happiness.

    We took some time apart after dating for a few years but after a few months, I realized that I didn't want to spend another moment without Mommy in my life, so I asked her to marry me and we planned to start our family. Everything was great... or so I thought. I knew that marriage was hard, and I

knew from the beginning that we'd have to work really hard to make it through. Still, I prayed for peace, love and happiness, but was missing peace and happiness while not loving one another how we needed. Love was there, but it was toxic. We knew love wasn't supposed to feel like that, so we made a choice.

Many times, we have to make difficult decisions for the betterment of ourselves and others. As we went through a process of heartache, pain, and deceit, we finally chose to split. A few years later, I realized that my process to achieve peace, love, and happiness, was for it to be taken so that we can truly appreciate it. Unfortunately, it wasn't meant for us to share those feelings with each other. Instead, we devoted the rest of our lives to make sure that you feel no void in the absence of peace, love, or happiness.

Mommy and Daddy felt guilty about the life we practically stole from you because we couldn't work things out, so we spoiled you in every way and we loved you even harder. We wanted to make sure that you didn't feel any of the horrible feelings we both felt. For me, it was complicated because as your father, I needed to be sure to instill certain qualities that only a man can do. Similarly, I'm certain your mother experienced different challenges in determining how she would teach you certain things that only a woman can teach. I'll never know, that's her story to tell. As it pertains to love from your Daddy, the first man in your life, I needed to find a balance and I call it stern and tender loving.

Stern and Tender Loving...

Stern and tender loving is essential in life.
Sometimes, I love you with a touch.
Sometimes, I love you with positive affirmation.
More often than not, I'll tell you with my lips
Though I know it matters mostly through my actions,
but it's OK, I'll always show you.
Tender to be, for my most precious gift,
Or stern at times to appropriately convey life's lessons.
I pray you can love me through both of these loves.
It's a mandated quality every man must possess to keep order.
One must not abuse it, but only implement this love when he sees fit.
One day, you will understand that as a king, I have been blessed to raise a princess that will one day transform into queen who will carefully choose her king.
And on that day, undoubtedly, I will have to give your hand in marriage.
I pray that you understand the equity of submission within that covenant,

And hopefully, you too, will be able to differentiate stern and tender loving to appreciate the nature of both beasts.

My love is tender, my love is stern,
If cold love is frowned upon, then know that for you, my love burns.

Baby, I don't have all the answers... I never did. But, I dedicate my life to finding them and doing the best I can to raise you and be engaged in your life. Never question if Daddy loves you! Sometimes, I may not respond appropriately, or say the very thing that you need, but if you know my heart, you'll always know that I mean well. If ever I make your heart cry, I promise I'll be the one to make it smile again. Some of my teachings won't be for you to understand immediately. In fact, there are some that you won't understand until you're grown and have a family of your own, but trust that most of my teachings are to elevate you to another level in life. I only pray that my stern and tender love was enough for you.

Flawed love, my lovely daughter. Although I love you with all I have, admittedly, I struggle in areas of loving you. Remember when I told you that it's important to learn how to love someone according to how they would receive it? It's important that you practice that concept every day because even as an adult at thirty years old, I still struggle with "getting it right." There are some days that I wish I hadn't said what I said, or did what I did as it pertained to you. That's why I call it flawed love. This means that someone can love you with all their heart and have every intention of protecting it, however, we are only human, and we are bound to make mistakes. I pray that you practice forgiveness. Forgive sooner rather than later, for it can haunt you and prevent growth from within, if you don't.

    As a healthcare professional, I'm very conscious and aware of chronic illnesses, bad habits that affect our health, and the effects of a neglected healthy practice for the body. When you were a baby, you came out chunky – cute chunky like no baby I had ever seen. I tried to watch what we as your parents fed you. Luckily, I was wise enough to know that proportions are everything when it comes to maintaining a certain weight. Since the 1970s, obesity has been on the rise and continues to increases at an alarming rate. This was another reason why your mother and I didn't see eye-to-eye. Often, when kids are brought into this world, they don't have control over what they eat or how much they eat while parents have increased proportions when feeding their kids. I promised to not do that to my own kids.

Now that I've given you a brief background, I'll explain why that has everything to do with flawed love. I found myself intentionally taking you on athletic outings with me so that you could grow up in a "fit" environment. My siblings and I grew up in a "fit" setting and we all have a nice physical appearance which defies the obesity rate in our country. Your mother, however, saw it as me being selfish and doing what I enjoy doing when I had my parenting time, but I was only emulating how I grew up. My father's interests became mine and my brother's interests and ours became his. There have been moments that I've openly mentioned that your tummy was pretty big, and I honestly didn't realize how those comments may impact you as you get older. Your mother brought it to my attention and I felt so terrible afterwards. I wish that I was able to take it back, but I can't. I've had numerous moments like that situation. I never meant to be malicious towards you or had intentions of hurting you - it was just me speaking out loud without realizing how it could affect others. Flawed love! I've learned my lesson. Not that it has an impact on you right now, but I realized that I needed to be more cognizant of what I said because I know how hearing something like that from a male, let alone your own Daddy, can influence your thought process as you get older.

    As I continue to learn how to love you, I still struggle with certain aspects of our new dynamic and our love. As Mommy and Daddy gain new friends and bring you around them, it's quite difficult to hear my daughter speak of another man in any capacity of love. Admittedly, there were times that I didn't respond how I should have and other times I didn't say anything, even when I should have. It's important to have peace among all parties when dealing with two separate homes, but as this is new to me and our family, there have been a few struggles with communication and you loving someone other than your Mommy and Daddy. I've grown, I've adapted, and I've prayed for a transformed heart to understand. I'm stronger and wiser, but most importantly, I know that I am Daddy. I will have to share your love, and I'm finding peace in that, but I trust in God that my love can and will never be replaced.

True Forgiveness

As you embark on your journey in your life, I emphatically encourage you to master the art of forgiveness. This is the only true method of sustaining some sort of relationship with the people in this world. Make no mistake, forgiveness doesn't mean you need to keep that person in your life, but be wise enough to know that truly forgiving someone is simply that you are at peace with the "wrong" they have committed to you. Let it go, and leave it to God. Continue to be open and connect with people despite any pain or grief anyone has caused you. Forgiveness will help you sustain fulfillment. Besides, who are you to not forgive with all the wrong you have done? Whether you're "wrong" was intentionally, or whether it's in secrecy. Look in the mirror, and find peace with yourself as well. God forgave us all for the sins we have committed and contemplate to commit. Forgiveness is effort, practice it every day of your life. Without adversity, you won't progress in life. Trials in your life will create resilience. Trust your process to become better and you'll never be lost.

Chapter 5: Know Your Worth

Worth...

Gold, pearls, and diamonds,
Where do you find them?
Are they easily visible?
Are their locations permissible?
Nothing on this earth can help the human eye magnify the visual.
Why? Because they are precious and rare.
Any person that owns one keeps them in cautious care.
What they are worth can sometimes be seen as priceless.
So, I write this...
To emulate the resemblance of their beauty as it relates to yours,
What they embody to this world.
They that define rich or poor,
You, an angelic little girl with so much meaning and worth,

The very gender that gives birth.

These items are hard to retrieve due to their location in this world.

Gold is deep in the earth from natural processes down to the core, pearls in an ocean, and diamonds deep in the core of the earth just as gold.

Every so often due to a natural disaster or tectonic plates colliding, some of these precious items surface so that they become visible or within reach of humans.

Like you, they are rare in form, scarce in beauty, and divine as such.

Conduct yourself accordingly because you are a unique gem on this earth.

Contain your goodies, secure your treasures, and only give yourself to the one who God deems worthy.

In your heart, you'll know, your mind will be aligned with your internal desires, and your heavenly spirit will keep you.

With everything in me, and my fatherly duties, as I'm only human, and make mistakes, but may you choose your complemented gem based on what I, your father, have shown you.

Baby, it's a cold world out there and trust me when I say that Daddy knows all the tricks. I stress to you, know your worth! There are so many young women out there who fall into the trap of young men that say words that sound like it's everything you need. In reality, however, it's just for temporary fulfillment. I pray that I have filled you with enough love that there are no voids in you. My love is enough. If my love isn't matched from the man that you deem worthy of being with, then he just isn't that - he isn't worthy. Compare my love to that of which you choose to date. If it is worthy, then I approve. If not, don't invest your heart.

Worthy...

A man will be dreamy
A man will tell you what you want to hear
Based on your curves,
It's all in his words.
Be wise enough to know if it's meant to be,
Be careful in judgement if it's heaven sent.
You are worthy!
Worthy of a gentleman
A man that gives you just what you need:
Respects you, invests in your mind,
You'll know when it's a rare breed
Trust what I taught you
Trust your instincts.
Never ignore your gut,
It's your Holy Spirit speaking to you
Don't confuse lust and love.
You are worthy,
Worthy of everything you desire
Never to be judged of your priors.
Never engage with a liar.
You are worthy.
Why?
Because Daddy says so and my word is enough
What I showed you was real love.

Chapter 6: Love Isn't Materialistic

Often, as humans, we tend to ignore action and focus on embellished articulations that come from the mouth or even materialistic gestures. Don't confuse them. While gifts are sweet and can be symbolic of a person's feelings, make note that actions should and must follow suite for finer things can be disguised with ill intentions that aren't in your best interest. Some people have motives that will break your heart in the end. Remember, you are worthy, you are rare, and if their treatment compares to mine towards you, then it just may be worthwhile. Seek me as your example, seek me as your guidance, and most of all, seek what my love exudes for you. Then, I can live in peace knowing that you have chosen your one based on my love and the standards I have set for you. I trust that my teachings will be enough.

Baby Pooh, it's important for you to find balance in getting what you want and need while also being able to receive the answer "no" to some of that. You are spoiled, so you may have a hard time dealing with not getting what you want. It's not your fault, though... it's mine and your mother's. With you being our only daughter, you've been immensely blessed with "things." Many of that is from your mother, admittedly, so be grateful for her desire to spoil you immensely. I've chosen to bless you with other things that you may appreciate later in life.

The amount of clothes you wear, the shoes you have, the toys in your rooms... I'm certain you can notice a difference between homes, but keep in mind that you have more than you need and a lot of what you want. Neither what I do, nor your mother, are doing things with ill intention, but rather for your best interest. Be thankful for your mother, I hope that you are as grateful for me as well. Her and I are a team and no matter what we go through in life, we'll always have one thing in common and that is you and the love we share for you.

If a man can't buy you things, don't eliminate him immediately. Seek his heart first. If he can buy you lavish things, be mindful of his intent and still seek his heart first. It's a double-edged sword and you must find the balance under both circumstances because some people think money can buy love and happiness. Happiness and joy, however, come from within. On the other hand, love is all around us and can even be disguised in many shapes and forms. The love your mother and I have instilled in you should be sufficient enough to overlook the material things.

    Be wise enough to understand that not only am I referring to your romantic love, but also love from friends and family. Look deep into the hearts that seek you, know their intent, and forgive misunderstood actions. Let your heart guide you and your mind consult you.

    As an infant as well as a toddler, you've been loved profusely by your family. With Mommy and Daddy living in the Chicago area, you've developed many close relationships with your Mommy's side of the family. I'm appreciative and grateful for the love they show you even though I've had to make sacrifices and do my due diligence to ensure you also have lasting relationships with my family that is in Tennessee. I once promised to take you down at least once a month and

I've done my best. I've sacrificed money and time, and I think you appreciate the times that we go to Tennessee because you love it so much and enjoy your time with Nana, Poppa, Uncle Brian, Titi Jasmine, Uncle Rob, Uncle Chris, Titi Donnie, Jasmia, JJ, Caleb, Jayden, Baby Brian, Baby Rob, and Kam. We also take annual trips to spend time with Titi Lala and Uncle Vince in California so that you can hang out with Junior in California. Likewise, wherever Tonka is, I make sure that you get time with him if he's in Tennessee or Chicago with Uncle E. We make time to see all our family throughout the Chicagoland area when we can, and you love it! As the family grows, do your part to ensure the family bond remains strong on both sides.

    Relationships with your cousins have always been the top of my priority list as you all grow up. Because you live in the same neighborhood as your cousins on Mommy's side, it's also important for you to take advantage of the blessing of having a big family, on both sides. I can only wish that you continue what we have tried to instill within you to sacrifice time to build relationships with your family. At the end of the day, family is all you have. Sometimes, family is extended beyond the nature of your blood, but the family that God has put in your life is a blended family.

Despite what it may seem in terms of family visiting you in Chicago, understand that it isn't as easy as it may seem. It took me a while to understand that. Though you may find that we take more trips out of state to visit family, know that the family is doing their unseen part to ensure a relationship is maintained as well. Let me give you a little background on Daddy's family.

To begin, Poppa served in the military for over 23 years. He served in countless wars while Nana stayed home, worked, and raised us during his time of sacrifice. After so many years in the military, Poppa was deemed 100% disabled form his service. Disabled, however, doesn't always mean that one can't walk or function... it's deeper than that. Poppa is highly educated and has a Bachelor's degree as well, but long trips to Chicago impact his health and prevent him and Nana from making other events to Chicago. You'll notice that most of the pictures you see with them are made in Tennessee, but I'm here to tell you that Poppa loved you dearly, baby.

As for Nana, Nana is a strong woman that exudes beauty and strength. She has not always shown affection or sympathy with raising four boys and one girl, but we now understand why she was the way that she was. She had to be strong and stern so that me and your uncles didn't run all over her. She definitely didn't play that! Nana adores you and loves you dearly. Your Nana has sickle cell anemia, a blood disorder that has a large impact on the African American community. It's genetically inherited and she has the dominant trait while your uncles and I all have the recessive trait. That simply means that we are carriers but don't experience symptoms like Nana.

Nana experiences pain often in her organs, tissues, and bones due to lack of oxygen in her blood cells. You are three right now and will be turning four in a few months. Nana has already undergone two hip replacements, two shoulder replacements, and other medical complications due to her disease. She has to stay home from work at times due to her pain she experiences, but Nana's love for you hasn't changed one bit and it isn't less than any other family member from both sides. Though Nana couldn't physically be present at times, her love is and has always been infinite and unconditional. She is one of the main reasons that Daddy was able to start over and rebuild a foundation for you and me. I encourage you to appreciate distant love.

Given the background and complications of your grandparents from Tennessee, I need you to understand that material things aren't important when it comes to love. Think deeper than that.

My Will, My Legacy

Tomorrow is not promised. I live for today, but plan for tomorrow. Should my time come unexpectedly, this book will give Robert Christopher Townsend Sr. direction on how to execute my Will.

1. Mia Amor Townsend is the heir of ALL my property/estates and is to be managed by Robert C. Townsend Sr. until she turns 18 years of age.
2. Robert C. Townsend Sr. as the primary beneficiary of all of my insurance plans (except 1 that is assigned to Stephanie A. Townsend) that he will use the funds to pay off any debt from my estates and property and use the remaining funds for all of Mia's expenses. $1,000 will be paid out to her

mother Stephanie, monthly to last until Mia is 18 years of age. The funds will then be paid directly to Mia in the same increments until she is 30. Upon her 30th birthday, the remaining of my insurance policy will be given to her in a lump sum for her own desires.

3. Mia's 529 College savings plan is already instructed for her educational endeavors.
4. Mia's UTMA (Uniform Transfers to Minors Act) through Primerica is to be used by Mia for whatever she desires at the age of 21. (House, wedding, car, etc).
5. Upon my death, all of my assets in my financial portfolio, including my 401K, all investment accounts should be withdrawn, (accepting all penalties associated) and will be transferred to Robert Christopher Townsend Sr., and included in Mia's lump sum when she turns 30 years of age on February 10th, of 2044.

Owner: _____

Witness: _____

Chapter 7: Your Love

Mia Amor, my love… oh, how I adore you.
How I love you, live for you… I'd die for you.
To express what your love has taught me,
I cannot express in words, but I tried.
My child, my daughter, my love,
My everything, my world.
Your love is undeniable, it's unconditional, and most of all, it's true.
True to who you are. It's the very thing that mends my heart yet also breaks it simultaneously. As I now have to share your love with another, I pray that you'll love me like no other.
I and only I, am your father, your Daddy, your provider. I hope to be the man you envision in your husband. I pray that you replicate my best qualities as a man and

seek that in yours. I hope that you also consider my worst qualities and seek to uplift your future husband to make him better than me so that he can treat you like the queen that you are.

A woman once told me that you have a big heart With lots of love to go around.

Selfishly, I want it all for me, but now I have to share. And since I must, I'll do my best to be open to love's many dynamics and I'll trust the process of loving abundantly. The very thing your mother and I did was love you harder to disguise any pain, and because of that, your heart is bigger than mine. Your love helped heal my heart and it saved my life. For that, this type of love needs to spread throughout the world. In each letter I've written, tears have fallen on my cheeks and as I conclude my letters, I'll end with a prayer:

"Dear Heavenly Father,

    I pray to you, Lord, keep my daughter and send your angles to protect her. I pray to you that my love was enough, and should she have any voids to fill, I pray that she seeks your love. I pray that when she goes through difficult times and develops ungodly habits, as we all do, I pray that she empties herself so that you can fill her up with your love. I pray that my love satisfies her and her relationship with you grows as her heavenly father. I thank you for allowing me to be her earthly father. I'm so grateful and appreciative of this opportunity for a little girl to call me Daddy, and not just any little girl, but THIS little girl we named Mia Amor. Lord, you know my heart. I pray that if given the opportunity to share our love with the world, we'll do so as long as I breath, but should you call me home prior to her reading this last letter, I pray that my little girl knows how I felt and that these were my most intimate thoughts that I'm sharing with her and the world. They will forever be engraved for her and I pray that my thoughts will forever warm her heart.

Amen"

Acknowledgements

I am deeply grateful and owe tremendous thanks to my unmet mentors, Pastor T.D. Jakes Sr., and American Motivational Speaker, Eric Thomas. Additionally, I would be remiss if I didn't show gratitude to my church based in Chicago, Illinois, House of Hope (Salem Baptist Church). In my darkest times, Pastor Jakes, and E.T.'s YouTube videos saved my life. They gave me strength when I was weak, and showed me light when it was dark. Some of my toughest moments in life were overcame from their sermons and words of wisdom to lift me up. I thank them with every ounce of my heart. House of Hope gave me a home when I was lost, and for that, I found the lord on my hands and knees asking for his grace. I also thank Kogut & Wilson LLC. Their guidance and support through this process to help me focus on the love for my daughter. Last but not least, I thank my daughter's mother who gave me a chance to know what real love felt like and also to ignite a type of love I never knew existed within me. Thank you all.

About the Author

Runnell Townsend Jr is the Founder of Runnell Jr & My Love LLC, an organization geared towards motivating, mentoring, inspiring, and empowering young men and fathers to love ourselves and overcome trials and tribulations we face in society that prevent us from infecting the world with our brotherly and fatherly love. Runnell is a student of life and seeks to make the world a better place through his passions. He's a healthcare professional finishing his PhD in Public Health at the University of Illinois @ Urbana-Champaign. Working full time at a Health System in the Chicagoland area, Runnell dedicates his life to eliminating health disparities and changing minority culture and the outlook about healthcare in the U.S. As the world becomes darker in times with less love, Runnell is determined to drive out darkness of hate, with the light of love. He recognizes the absence of fathers in the household. He's determined to empower, encourage and motivate fathers to play their part, regardless of their circumstance. Runnell is determined to infect the world with love by opening his life with his daughter for the world to see.

Contact Runnell Townsend Jr

Email: **runnelljrandmylove@gmail.com**

Instagram: runnelljrandmylove

Facebook:

www.facebook.com/runnelljrandmylove/

Website: MyLoveEmpowers.com

For bookings regarding motivational speaking at your University, or organization, please email me at the listed address above.

"Loving one another, even when it hurts"

-Runnell Jr

www.ingramcontent.com/pod-product-compliance
Lightning Source LLC
Chambersburg PA
CBHW051957290426
44110CB00015B/2278